It was the day before Christmas. Brother Vivvy, Rich, Kirsten and Tom, were in a h

Their Mum and Dad were shopping in the town near the cottage.

But Mum and Dad phoned them. Kirsten answered it.

'They can't get back. There's too much snow. They're staying at a hotel in town tonight,' Kirsten said.

They all thought it was terrible. Christmas with no Mum
and Dad! And they weren't in their house. They were in
a holiday cottage in the snow!

'OK,' Tom said.
'We'll have Christmas by ourselves. Come on! Let's decorate the room.'

'Let's make some Christmas food,' Kirsten said.

'We can play with our toys,' Rich said.

'And let's decorate the tree!' Vivvy said.

'Father Christmas won't know we're here and won't come!' Vivvy said.

'I know,' Rich said. 'We'll write him a letter and put it up the chimney.'

So they did!

They were hungry and they all made dinner – a brilliant Christmas pizza with red and green peppers, cheese, tomatoes and ham.

'It's the best pizza in the world,' they said.

'Let's watch TV,' Vivvy said.
There were two silly old men on the TV dressed like
Father Christmases, dancing about. It made everyone
laugh and laugh… they could not stop.

'Let's find something funny to wrap up for each other for tomorrow,' Kirsten said.

So they all found and wrapped some little presents for each other for Christmas Day.

Tom found some torches and they all went outside to play in the garden. They started to throw snowballs at each other in the dark!

It was great!

Then they made a snowman with two big, big
snowballs. One had a face made of things from
the garden. It looked brilliant.

They were wet and cold but happy.

Next morning it was Christmas Day.

They all came downstairs very early…

…and opened their funny presents.

They played with their toys…

…and ate chocolate things for breakfast!

After that they all got dressed…

…and went outside to play in the snow again.

Suddenly, Rich said, 'He came! He came! Father Christmas came!'

There were presents for each of them!

They went inside to open their presents. Vivvy got paints, Tom got books, Rich got a computer game and Kirsten got a kite.

'It's time for a party,' Kirsten said.

12

They listened to music, opened Christmas crackers, put on the silly hats and told some terrible jokes.

'What's black and white and read all over?' Tom said. 'A newspaper!'

Suddenly, they heard the door. It was Mum and Dad!

'Mum, Dad, we had snowball fights, chocolate for breakfast and lots of presents,' Vivvy said.
'It was the best Christmas!'

Activities

Before you read

1. Look at the picture on page 9.
   Can you see a snowman?
   Draw a picture of the snowman.

2. How many children are
   in this story?

After you read

Look at the presents in the book and find four presents you like.

Here is a letter Vivvy wrote to Father Christmas.

> Dear Father Christmas,
>
> I'd like some paints for Christmas please.
> I'd like some chocolate too
> Thank you
> Vivvy

Now write your own letter to Father Christmas.

Pearson Education Limited
Edinburgh Gate, Harlow,
Essex CM20 2JE, England
and Associated Companies throughout the world.

ISBN 978-0-582-34408-2

10
First published 2000
Penguin Books
© Text copyright Annie Hughes 2000
© Illustrations Megumi Biddle 2000

Design by Jim Wilkie, J and R Press

Printed in China
SWTC/10

Published by Pearson Education Limited in association with Penguin Books Ltd,
both companies being subsidiaries of Pearson Plc

For a complete list of titles available in the Penguin Readers series please write
to your local Pearson Education office or contact: Penguin Readers Marketing
Department, Penguin Education, Edinburgh Gate, Harlow, Essex, CM20 2JE.